TENERIFE

Gomera • La Palma • El Hierro

Ken Bernstein

GW00722381

J·P·M

PUBLICATIONS

CONTENTS

This Way Tenerife

Emblem of the Isles

You see it from the air, hundreds of kilometres before you land in the Canaries—Tenerife's Mount Teide, poking above the clouds like a softly rounded beacon. Chances are that the topmost slopes are covered in snow, even though this is the land of eternal springtime. The sight has startled travellers over the centuries. Columbus's crew saw volcanic sparks and smoke billowing from the peak and worried that it was a hellish omen for their first voyage beyond the map.

At more than 3,700 m (over 12,000 ft), Tenerife's mountain is the highest in all of Spain, yet hundreds of thousands of tourists reach the summit every year—with the help of a cable car. The biggest of the Canaries in area, Tenerife can offer something for everyone: beaches, forests, subtropical plantations, plus an intriguing history, a unique culture, plenty of nightlife, and every luxury a tourist could demand. Somewhere beyond the big-time resorts, the real Tenerife awaits your discovery.

Blessed and Beautiful

Seven Fortunate Islands emerge from the Atlantic Ocean, stepping stones from North Africa into what, until five centuries ago, was the great unknown. The ancients imagined that somewhere out there was the Garden of the Hesperides, the Elysian Fields, or Atlantis—in any case a place blessed and beautiful. This undiscovered string of volcanic pearls would surely have fitted the bill.

In the middle of the archipelago, Tenerife stands supreme, yet it's only two-thirds the size of Majorca (another Spanish island that's immensely popular with tourists). This guide also covers Tenerife's lesser-known satellite islands: green and hilly Gomera, delightful La Palma and the smallest and least populous Canary, El Hierro, last stop before America. The four western islands have so much in common that they have constituted a separate province since 1927.

The Earth Moved

Millions of years ago the crunch came when the tectonic plates forming the earth's crust yielded to the strain. As the foundations of Africa and South America edged apart, slabs under the Atlantic reared up, releasing explosions of molten rock. Lava-spewing volcanoes solidified into

Terraces of bananas descend to a hamlet near Tenerife's north coast.

the Canary Islands. The eruptions still go on from time to time, although nothing worth headlines has happened since 1971 on La Palma. Stay tuned.

On all the islands, the volcanic soil produces rich dividends in fruit and vegetables, such as tomatoes and bananas, rushed to eager markets in Europe. To get a jump on the competition, improvised hothouses of plastic sheeting disfigure some areas of the countryside. Less known abroad, the mini-potatoes are smaller than golf balls and irresistibly tasty, savoured skin and all. They are customarily doused in a piquant sauce of local invention.

Gofio and Guanches

The staff of life in the Canaries is *gofio,* a powdery mixture of milled, toasted grains used to thicken soups, stews and sauces. *Gofio* was the staple food of the mysterious indigenous people who inhabited all seven principal islands when the 15th-century Spanish conquerors came along.

The aborigines of Tenerife were called Guanches; the name is, by extension, often used for the first inhabitants of the other islands. When the Spaniards decided to exploit the archipelago, they first planted the flag on the island closest to Europe, Lanzarote. But they soon realised that the other islands had to be taken by force. Fortunately for Columbus, Gran Canaria had fallen to Ferdinand and Isabella just in time for his fleet to stop for supplies in 1492. But the *Niña,* the *Pinta* and the *Santa María* gave Tenerife a wide berth; the Stone Age Guanches were still fighting for their freedom.

Getting Your Bearings

On the map, Tenerife is shaped something like a broody hen. Around the feet, in the south, are the intercontinental airport, the most extensive beaches and the main tourist resorts. These are linked to the island's capital, near the level of the chicken's neck, by a modern motorway. Santa Cruz de Tenerife, with a population of more than 204,000, is as likeable and stately as any city of its size in Spain. On the opposite side of the island, Puerto de la Cruz was the first Canaries resort, attracting health-seeking European tourists late in the 19th century. All but beachless, it now compensates with an inspired, man-made, semi-tropical sea-front. In the north it may be chilly and rainy, but you can be sure sunbathers are out in force on the southern beaches. Dividing the two mini-climates, Mount Teide rises to the heavens, an ever-present influence—meteorological, geological and spiritual.

Flashback

Scenes from History

The great names of antiquity knew and raved about the archipelago, or so claim confident Canarians. Homer, they insist, must have been referring to these very islands when he wrote in the *Odyssey* about the eternally happy, winterless Elysian Fields. In the *Aeneid,* they say, Virgil meant the Canaries when he described the "fortunate islands", a sort of retirement home for the virtuous. The historian Herodotus told of the idyllic Garden of the Hesperides, and the well-travelled Plutarch mentioned paradise isles off Africa basking in eternal springtime—they could only be the Canaries, obviously.

After this powerful boost for the archipelago's image, the Canaries somehow slipped from the world's view for more than a thousand years. The first European navigators to set foot on these enviable beaches arrived in the 14th century. Oddly, they didn't tend to linger. Perhaps the inhabitants didn't make them feel welcome.

Mountainous vistas in the north of Tenerife, near Bajamar.

Cavemen

All seven of the main islands were inhabited well before European explorers arrived on the scene. The indigenous population, generally called Guanches after the name of the aborigines of Tenerife, were literally cavemen. They are thought to have emigrated from North Africa in the 1st or 2nd centuries BC, and they spoke a Berber language. But it's a mystery how they managed to overcome the perils of the Atlantic when they apparently knew nothing about boats or navigation. Their Stone Age lifestyle wasn't quite as primitive as might be expected. One of their most remarkable achievements was the mastery of a sophisticated technique for mummifying their dead. They had a form of tribal government. They made inscriptions in stone; the meanings of most of them have never been deciphered. Another curiosity: the Guanches were tall in stature, light-skinned, blond and often blue-eyed. The clues tantalize ethnologists and others who like a puzzle. The Guanches who weren't wiped out during the Spanish Conquest were eventually assimilated into the new Canary society.

Europeans

Early in the 14th century the first European influences arrived in the Canaries, starting on the black volcanic island of Lanzarote. In 1312, it's thought, a Genoese traveller, Lancelote Malocello, gave his name to the island, but he didn't stay. Another version attributes the name of Lanzarote to a later arrival, a Frenchman called Lancelot. And there is yet another explanation: when Jean de Béthencourt had subdued the aborigines early in the 15th century, he may have broken his lance as a symbol of peace, and declaimed, *"Lanza rota!"* (broken lance). Whatever the story, Lanzarote, the island closest to Europe, was the first to fall. The pacification effort across the archipelago took nearly all of the 15th century. The mopping-up hadn't even been completed when the Canaries became the springboard for Columbus and those who followed him to the New World.

The Guanches had reason to be wary of the conquering Spaniards. For years Europeans had been sending raiding parties to collect slaves; some of the islands were almost depopulated by the 15th century. In 1496, the last holdout of the valiant Guanches of Tenerife fell to the Spanish crown. The cavemen embraced Christianity and most elements of Spanish culture, and within a century or two no discernible difference remained between natives and colonists. But traces of Guanche culture remain in everyday life: distinctive festivals, recipes, sports, and, on the island of Gomera, a whistling language for communicating from hill to hill.

Columbus Day

Christopher Columbus and his expedition set forth from Palos de la Frontera, in southwestern Spain, on August 3, 1492, in search of the "Indies". He didn't try to do the Atlantic nonstop.

1

THE BEST TREE In the forests and valleys of Tenerife, trees as varied as pines and palms proliferate. But one rare old tree stands out: the giant dragon tree of **Icod de los Vinos,** west of Puerto de la Cruz, which may be 3,000 years old. Its tightly packed maze of branches with razor-sharp leaves never fails to fascinate. No wonder the aboriginal Guanches considered dragon trees sacred.

First he pulled in at Gran Canaria for repairs, supplies and some rest. He bypassed Tenerife, where battles between Guanches and Spaniards were still under way. Next and last stop: Gomera, to top up the food and water rations, and for prayers at the Church of Our Lady of the Assumption. On September 6, the convoy took off into the unknown. Finally, on October 12, a crewman sighted land—America, as it turned out.

A triumphant Columbus was back in the Canaries on his voyages of 1493 and 1498; they say the real attraction on Gomera was not so much the food, water and prayers as the hospitality of Beatriz de Bobadilla, beautiful widow of the governor.

Economic Affairs

During the Golden Age of the Spanish empire, the Canaries became an important port of call for the increasing transatlantic traffic. Tales of fabulous riches convinced many islanders to join the colonists heading for new lives in Latin America. (Pioneers from Tenerife founded the cities of Montevideo, Uruguay, and San Antonio, Texas.) But the boom in the New World proved a setback for Canaries farmers: their sugar was priced out of the European market, for the West Indian equivalent was produced by slave labour.

A BIRD IN HAND

No, the Canary Islands are not named after the world's most popular pet bird. On the contrary, your feathered friend is named after the archipelago, of which it is a native. *Serinus canarius*, to be formal, is a small finch whose charm is in its song. The colourful plumage is a bit of genetic engineering. Since the 16th century, when canaries became favourite caged pets in Europe, dozens of new varieties have been bred, with ever more original colours. For the record, only the male canary can sing.

Luckily for the Canaries, Europeans acquired a taste for malmsey (*malvasía*) wine, with a rich flavour attributed to the volcanic soil in which the grapes are grown. Soon island vineyards were working with all deliberate speed to produce the sweet white wine that would grace the best tables in London and Paris.

Nelson's Arm

A distinguished visitor came calling at Tenerife in 1797. At the time, Spain was allied with France in hostilities against England. Horatio Nelson, who would go on to become England's greatest naval hero, led a raid on the port of Santa Cruz de Tenerife in the hope of capturing some Spanish ships laden with colonial booty. The defenders of Santa Cruz responded in force, inflicting hundreds of casualties on the attackers. One lucky shot took off Nelson's right arm. (In Santa Cruz today you can see the cannon in question.) Santa Cruz de Tenerife won the titles of Very Loyal, Noble and Invincible city. Nelson more than evened the score in 1805, defeating the combined fleets of Spain and France at Trafalgar. But in the moment of his greatest triumph the one-eyed, one-armed admiral was killed in action.

Duty Free

In 1852 a royal decree from Madrid transformed the Canary Islands into one big free port. It was a bold move to strengthen the islands' economy by encouraging more international trade. Boom times came to the ports of Santa Cruz de Tenerife and Las Palmas de Gran Canaria, which went on to gain great significance in world trade. Their cosmopolitan vitality remains impressive. And some of the prices of imported luxury goods still delight visiting shoppers.

Franco Swoops

In 1936 the captain-general of the Canary Islands was Francisco Franco, a bright, young, ambitious Spanish general. Despairing of the state of the nation under the Republican government in Madrid, Franco called together like-minded officers for a secret meeting in a Tenerife forest. Here was conceived the uprising that ignited the Spanish Civil War. Franco won the war, which cost hundreds of thousands of lives. The wily dictator was able to maintain a neutral Spain during World War II and gain entry to the United Nations in 1955.

Europe Calls

On Franco's death in 1975, the successor he had designated, the young Prince Juan Carlos de Borbón, took over the long-vacant Spanish throne. He presided over the restoration of democracy and a drastic improvement in the attitude to the country's regional peculiarities. The Canaries, for instance, became an autonomous region with a local parliament. On the international scene, after decades as an outcast, democratic Spain became a pillar of the European Union and the economy boomed.

Meanwhile, Canaries tourism grew to mass market proportions as more and bigger jets brought holidaymakers to the fortunate isles of eternal springtime, clear seas, and inviting beaches of golden, pink or black sand.

On the Scene

In other parts of the world you'd have to travel thousands of miles to see so many kinds of landscape. Tenerife reveals a snowy mountain, refreshing forests, volcanic badlands, semi-tropical plantations, desert and dramatic seascapes—all in a hard day's drive. (The roads range from six-lane motorway to hair-raising mountain zigzags.) The towns, too, are picturesque and rich in history, starting with the island's capital, an unhurried, palm-shaded city of more than 200,000.

TENERIFE

Santa Cruz de Tenerife, The North, Puerto de la Cruz, West of Puerto, Teide, Around the Coast

Santa Cruz de Tenerife

Although Santa Cruz de Tenerife is one of the busiest ports in Spain, it has surprisingly few tourists. While swarms of "sun birds" fly in to the south, Santa Cruz remains an unspoiled provincial capital with highrises and tasteful villas, distinguished official buildings and plenty of outdoor cafés. Founded at the end of the 15th century, the city was soon eclipsed by La Laguna, 5 km (3 miles) inland, hence safer from pirate attacks. Finally, with the decline of the pirate business, Santa Cruz was crowned as provincial capital of all the Canaries in 1821, a title it held for more than a century.

Plaza de España

Considering the city's vocation for international trade, it's natural that the centre of Santa Cruz is alongside the port. A 16th-century fortress was pulled down to make way for Plaza de España, which surrounds a big traffic roundabout with a monument in the middle—a four-sided cross honouring Spain's Civil War dead, erected during the Franco era. Plaza de España is where Tenerife's huge annual Carnival reaches its unrestrained climax. In quieter times, the plaza and the adjoining Plaza de la Candelaria are fine for strolling and relaxing at outdoor cafés, much patronized by the locals, sailors and tourists.

TENERIFE

Pu
C

San Juan
de la Rambla
Los
Realejos

Buenavista
del Norte
Los
Silos
Garachico
San
Marcos

Faro de Teno
El Tanque
Icod de
los Vinos
La
Guancha
Icod
el Alto

Macizo
de Teno
San Juán
del Reparo

Punta
de Teno
Las
Portelas
Erjos
San José
de los Llanos
Valle de la Oro

Masca
Montaña
de Abeque
1764 m
Pico de las
Cabras
2363 m
Centro de
Visitantes

Caldera de las Cañada

Tamaimo
Arguayo
Pico
del Teide
3717 m
Col
23

Los Gigantes
Los Gigantes
Pico Viejo
3134 m
Teleférico
Parqu

Chío
Guía de
Isora
Cañada de
los Azulefos
Nacion
del Tei

Alcalá
Zapato de
la Reina

San Juán
Tejina

Tijoco
de Abajo
Barranco del
Infierno
Vilaflor
Las
Vaegas

Playa Paraiso
Adeje
Escalona
Charco
del Pino
Chi

El Puertito
Fañabé
Gran
de At

La Caleta
Arona
San
Miguel

Playa de
las Americas
Buzanada
Aeropuerto
Reina Sofia

Los Cristianos

Palm-Mar
Las
Galletas
Costa del
Silencio
Mé

La Gomera
Faro de la Rasca
Costa d

Roque de Fuera

Roque de Tierra

Punta
del Hidalgo

Taganana

Benijo

Chamorga

☆ **Faro de Anaga**

Lomo de las
Bodegas

Bajamar

Tejina

*Mirador Pico
del Inglés*
☆

Igueste

Valle
de Guerra

Tegueste

Las Montañas de Anaga

Playa de las
Teresitas

Mesa del Mar

Guamasa

San Andrés

La Palma - Madeira - La Gomera

El Sauzal

Tacoronte

San Cristóbal de
La Laguna

Matanza
centejo

Aeropuerto de Tenerife
Los Rodeos

**Santa Cruz
de Tenerife**

Victoria
centejo

☆
**Madre
del Aqua**

La Esperanza

Gran Canaria - Cádiz
Lanzarote - Fuerteventura

nta
rsula

*Mirador
Ortuño*

El Tablero

Orotava

Mirador Pico
de la Flores
☆

824

Barranco
Hondo

Tabaiba

Igueste

☆ *Mirador
de Chipeque*

Candelaria

vatorio
ómico
de

Arafo

El Socorro

zana
387 m

Güimar

n

Lomo
de Mena

Puerto de Güimar

1

Fasnia

El Tablado

arza

822

Fondeadero
de Fasnia

Viejo
Nuevo

Poris de Abona

no
Arico

☆ *Faro de Abona*

Sanatorio
de Abona

San Miquel de Tajao

Callao del Rio

ilencio

N

0   10 km

A national monument on the pedestrians-only Plaza de la Candelaria is the Palacio Carta, a beautifully restored 18th-century palace in traditional Canaries style, now a bank.

Cabildo Insular

The monumental 1930s home of the Island Council faces Plaza de España. On the ground floor, a tourist information office is loaded with maps and brochures and has well-informed staff to answer every query.

Iglesia de la Concepción

Near the seafront, the slim bell-tower of the Church of the Immaculate Conception has been a landmark for approaching navigators since the 18th century, but the church itself was founded three centuries earlier.

Inside the church, which has been restored several times, are many highly esteemed works of art—paintings, gold- and silverware, woodwork, sculptures—together with a number of historic mementoes: most crucially the wooden Cross of the Conquest, dating from the earliest Spanish days.

Museo de la Naturaleza y el Hombre

The Museum of Nature and Man is housed in the old civil hospital (Antiguo Hospital Civil), a neo-classical building on Bravo Murillo Street, on the far side of the ravine called the Barranco de Santos.

The lifestyle of the Guanches, the island's original inhabitants, is documented here in every imaginable way—and in ways almost unimaginable, too. More than a thousand prehistoric skulls are lined up in neat rows in glass cases; they were much studied and measured in the days before carbon dating and other sophisticated research techniques. Here, too, lie Tenerife mummies, perfectly preserved proof of the aboriginal expertise in postmortem niceties. Less doleful are the displays of Guanche jewellery, costumes and utensils.

Teatro Guimerá

In the 19th century, visiting opera companies began stopping off at the Guimerá Theatre, usually on their way from Spain to engagements in Latin America. Oozing with decorative touches, the theatre was restored in the early 1990s. Here you may catch a performance of *zarzuela,* the usually light-hearted Spanish version of opera, or a play, or a concert by the Tenerife Symphony Orchestra or visiting musicians.

Museo de Bellas Artes

Facing the well-shaded park of the Plaza del Príncipe, in a small street with the quaint name of Calle José Murphy, the Municipal Museum of Fine Arts is ensconced above the 100,000-volume Municipal Library. Most of the well-displayed paintings here are by local artists, but José de Ribera, Federico de Madrazo and Joaquín Sorolla are also represented. Here, too, are sculptures and musical instruments.

Las Ramblas

In a traffic-choked city it's unusual to find cars and pedestrians coexisting, but they do nicely in the long boulevard known as Las Ramblas, lined with distinguished old and new buildings. The pedestrian area, separating two heavily travelled roadways, is comfortably shaded, equipped with benches and kiosks, and decorated with modern sculptures, most famously by Henry Moore and Joan Miró.

About halfway along the Ramblas stands the century-old municipal bullring. Because of a lack of local enthusiasm for the *fiesta brava,* and the high cost of transporting bulls, horses and bullfighters from the mainland, it has been several decades since a matador has been seen in action here. Instead the bullring is a venue for pop concerts and sports events.

Parque García Sanabria

The longest stretch of the boulevard is named la Rambla del General Franco. Other cities in Spain have erased Franco's personality cult but Santa Cruz remains true to the *caudillo,* who plotted his uprising in a secret meeting on the island.

Just off the Rambla del General Franco, a coolly shaded city park gives office workers a perfect respite from their daily pressures. El Parque García Sanabria, named after a popular mayor of Santa Cruz, is a pleasing mixture of landscaping and artistic effort. Along the pathways are fountains, flowerbeds, modern sculptures, monuments to local dignitaries, and a floral clock. Birds chatter excitedly in the mighty trees.

15

A remarkable tree: the legendary dragon tree of Icod.

Museo Militar Regional

The star attraction in the regional military museum, housed in a castle near the confluence of the Ramblas and the waterfront Avenida de Francisco La Roche, is a cannon. Nicknamed "El Tigre" (the tiger), this is the gun that is supposed to have hit the Royal Navy's Horatio Nelson when he besieged the city in 1797 and said farewell to his arm. The museum also features battle flags captured from the defeated English host. Other, less celebrated weapons, battle flags and uniforms fill out the museum's roomy quarters in the Castillo de Almeida.

Las Teresitas

As an international port full of freighters, tankers, container ships, fishing factory ships, trawlers and yachts, Santa Cruz has no waterfront left over for beaches. But 9 km (6 miles) northeast of the city, Las Teresitas has everything the beach-lover could want: about a mile of glorious golden sand, safe swimming, the shade of palm trees, and refreshment opportunities.

Only one false note: although the ocean was always there, that golden sand didn't arrive until 1970. It was mined in the (former Spanish) Sahara and shipped over, to upgrade an unimpressive pebbly stretch of coast. Break-waters were built to keep the new sand from drifting away. The beach is a good place to see the locals at leisure; they arrive by bus, car, motorbike and bicycle.

The North

The *autopista del norte* (northern motorway) climbs steeply from near sea level in Santa Cruz into the stark mountains that separate the capital from Tenerife's interior. The new route makes short work of the link between Santa Cruz and the traditional resort of Puerto de la Cruz, once a hard slog on twisting roads.

La Laguna

Surrounded by mountains that reduced the risk of invasion, La Laguna was chosen as the first capital of Tenerife by the Spanish conquerors, a distinction that lasted until the 19th century. It's still the island's ecclesiastical and cultural capital. The religious power is visible in the cathedral, seat of the diocese of Tenerife; culturally the distinction is spread around the university, encompassing traditional fields of study and an astrophysical institute.

La Laguna also has a museum of science and space. And in the old parts of this lively city of 125,000, there are fine traditional Canaries-style buildings worth seeing.

Alongside the *autopista,* on the edge of town, a giant bronze statue honours José de Anchieta, a 16th-century Jesuit priest from La Laguna, who founded the city of São Paulo.

Santa Iglesia Catedral

There's been a church on this site since 1511, but the present, imposing cathedral is a product of the 20th century. When the old building was discovered to be falling into ruin in 1897 they saved the neoclassical façade and began all over again. The neo-Gothic structure preserves historic works of art, including wood-carvings by the great 18th-century Canaries sculptor José Luján Pérez.

Iglesia de la Concepción

An austere 17th-century seven-storey bell tower stands over Tenerife's oldest parish church, the Church of the Immaculate Conception. Corpus Christi was celebrated here for the first time in 1496; the festival is still a very special occasion in La Laguna, when flowers decorate the streets. The church, a national monument, contains a beautifully carved baroque pulpit and a baptismal font brought from Seville by the island's conqueror and first governor, Alonso Fernández de Lugo. He's buried in the cathedral.

17

Los Rodeos

On the opposite side of the *autopista* from La Laguna, Los Rodeos airport, now known as Tenerife Norte, handles mostly inter-island flights, just a small fraction of Tenerife's air traffic. This was the island's first airport, inaugurated in 1941. Los Rodeos went into the history books in the most tragic way in 1977 when two commercial jumbo-jets collided on its runways, with a death toll of 583—the world's worst-ever civil air disaster.

Off the Motorway

Northeastward from La Laguna, increasingly tortuous roads climb into the cool, mysterious forest of Monte de las Mercedes. According to the altitude, laurel, beech and pine dominate. Along the way, *miradores* (lookout points) with ever more sensational vistas break the trip. The ultimate *mirador* is at Pico del Inglés (Englishman's peak), altitude 992 m (3,255 ft).

From here you can see the power of the Atlantic at Punta del Hidalgo and, in the opposite direction, the waves lapping at Las Teresitas.

Bajamar

For many years the people of La Laguna had Bajamar, just west of Punta del Hidalgo, to themselves. This is where they took their summer holidays by the sea. Now luxury hotels and holiday flats have gone up, assuring some international attention. Bajamar is one of those almost beachless Tenerife resorts that has made the most of its predicament, constructing artificial pools at the water's edge. At high tide the water refreshes itself. There's an agreeable seaside promenade.

Tacoronte

Wine-lovers won't want to miss Tacoronte, the centre of the largest area of vineyards in the Canary Islands. (The vines are elevated on trellises; underneath, they grow winter potatoes.) The Tacoronte-Acentejo area was the first zone in the archipelago to achieve the category of Denomination of Origin, classing the wines among the choicest regions in Spain. Dozens of wine-cellars await the visiting connoisseur, and there is a wine museum. Tacoronte's parish church spotlights a famous 17th-century statue of *Cristo de los Dolores* (Christ of the Sorrows). Another local church, Santa Catalina, is crammed with works of art.

La Matanza

The town's name is, to say the least, uninviting. La Matanza means "the massacre". Here, in 1494, the Spanish conquerors met their Waterloo. The Guanches,

18

THE NORTH • PUERTO DE LA CRUZ

armed with nothing but Stone Age weapons and knowledge of the countryside, ambushed the invaders in a deep ravine, raining down stones, spears and clubs. Captain Alonso Fernández de Lugo lost four-fifths of his troops. The survivors fled to Gran Canaria to recuperate and re-group. When they returned to Tenerife the following year the Guanches, weakened by the fight-ing as well as diseases imported from Spain, couldn't resist. Near the same ravine, Fernández de Lugo had his revenge, and a famous victory. Which is why the village down the road is called, more optimistically, La Victoria.

Puerto de la Cruz

In the 18th century, the malmsey wines of Tenerife were shipped from Puerto de la Cruz to the enthusiastic tipplers of England. In the 19th century, word got around that the climate of Puerto de la Cruz was therapeutic, and British doctors earnestly recom-mended that their patients take an all-purpose cure beside the Atlantic in the eternal springtime. Soon grand hotels and gardens transformed the old port into an international resort. Even when cured, the travellers kept coming back for more, as holidaymakers continue to do; the percentage of repeat visitors is one of the town's proudest statistics.

STRICTLY SPEAKING

The aboriginal inhabitants of Tenerife are called Guanches, and sometimes the name is ex-tended to the natives of other islands. But, strictly speaking, the cavemen of La Gomera were Gomeros, La Palma's aborigines were Auaritas, and El Hierro's Bimbaches. There's a lot of cultural overlap, but the Stone Age people of each is-land had their own vocabulary, customs and particularities.

On the Waterfront

Puerto de la Cruz—familiarly known as Puerto—has always been in the rather awkward posi-tion of a beach resort with almost no beach. Along much of the local coastline the Atlantic crashes ashore on the rocks except where it meets a small rocky cove packed with fishing boats, leaving a stretch of black volcanic sand beach, vulnerable to heavy tides and too small for all the tourist requirements.

Enter César Manrique (1919–92), the brilliant Lanzarote artist, architect and landscape designer who devised Costa Martiánez, a glamorous recreational facility stretching into the sea. With its big salt lake and seven lesser swimming pools, sunbathing areas, fountains and gardens, this is a festive, tasteful solution to the old problem. An island in the middle of the "lake" harbours a restaurant and, below sea level, a nightclub. For sand-lovers there's even a small protected beach, facing away from the incoming waves.

Two Churches

A small white chapel overlooking the ocean at the edge of the Martiánez complex, the Ermita de San Telmo is a fishermen's church, founded in 1780. The saint is supposed to look after storm-tossed sailors. In a sign of the times, masses are scheduled in German as well as Spanish.

The late-17th-century Iglesia de Nuestra Señora de la Peña de Francia (church of Our Lady of the Rock of France) is altogether more majestic. Among many other works of art, valuable polychrome wood sculptures adorn the chapels and niches. The statue of the Virgin of Carmen is much revered by local fishermen.

Plaza del Charco

Puerto's main square is where the locals go to sit in the shade and exchange gossip or play chess. Tourists, too, take advantage of the concentration of cafés, shops and restaurants, and there is a play area for children. The fishing port is virtually across the street, and the arrival of the boats al-ways stirs some excitement among potential buyers of the freshest of fresh fish. An overflow of boats is double-parked on the pavement above the beach.

Overlooking the fishing port, the Casa de la Real Aduana (Royal Customs House), dating from 1620, is considered the oldest building in town. The architecture is typically Canarian. It's been retired from the customs service for the last century-and-a-half.

West of Centre

Nearly a kilometre to the west, the 17th-century Castillo de San Felipe (castle of St Philip) was one of three forts that defended the town in pirate days. It looks out on a new beach area, Playa Jardín (Garden Beach), which lives up to its name. Backed by lush gardens and dotted with palm trees, the sandy beach is protected from the dangerous tides by a man-made reef. Farther west, Loro Parque, Tenerife's big bird park, has branched out into dolphins, and even gorillas, reptiles, sharks and bats. The birds represent a couple of hundred species, and some of them are star performers, with talents well beyond flying and singing.

Parque Taoro

On a promontory overlooking the sea and the city, the first luxury hotels for foreign health faddists, mostly British, were built in the 1890s. Taoro Park retains its dignity and its international character. Close at hand are an English library, an English school and an Anglican church (now at the disposal of various faiths and nationalities). The traditional Gran Hotel Taoro has been converted into a luxurious casino, where all the popular international games of chance are available. You have to present your passport to enter; the casino's computer tries to keep out notorious bad-cheque artists, as well as geniuses blacklisted for having broken the bank in Las Vegas or Monte Carlo.

Jardín Botánico

Much of Tenerife is a garden, a rainbow of mimosa, poinsettia and bougainvillea, of wild honeysuckle and carefully tended frangipani. On the edge of Puerto de la Cruz, the Botanical Garden has been taking the flora seriously for more than two centuries. Officially named the Acclimatisation Garden, it was founded by a royal decree of King Carlos III. The motive was to study exotic plants imported from Asia and Latin America and permit them a transition period before trying to grow them in the royal gardens of mainland Spain. (It wasn't easy, what with freezing winters in Madrid.)

Save an hour for tropical escapism in the shade of some amazing trees, such as a giant variety of fig tree from South America and the *jipijapa,* used in its homeland for the fabrication of Panama hats.

La Bananera el Guanche

Many of the banana plantations of the Puerto de la Cruz area have given way to tourist development. The Guanche Banana Plantation has combined the two vocations: it grows bananas and entertains tourists. At this plantation, between Puerto and La Orotava, the mystical life cycle of the banana plant is explained and there are tastings of bananas and banana liqueur. Other tropical fruits like pineapple, mango and papaya grow here, too, along with sugar cane and cactus.

La Orotava

Nowhere is Tenerife more green and fertile than in the Orotava Valley, a sight that so moved the German naturalist Alexander von Humboldt that he is said to have fallen to his knees in gratitude to God. The city of La Orotava, businesslike but alluring, is noted for its "floral carpets" that ennoble the streets for the Corpus Christi holiday. The steep, hilly streets lead to classical Canaries sights, none more widely photographed than the 17th-century

Casa de los Balcones, now a handicrafts centre. Finely carved balconies surround the internal patio, rich in subtropical atmosphere. The artefacts on display and the chance to watch local lace-makers and embroiderers make this an inevitable tourist stop. Across the street, the Casa del Turista dates from 1590.

Iglesia de la Concepción

The grandeur of La Orotava's baroque Church of the Immaculate Conception reflects the importance the city had in the 18th century, when Puerto de la Cruz was still known as Puerto de la Orotava. Actually, construction of the first church on this site began early in the 16th century, but an earthquake demolished it. The present church, a national monument, was consecrated in 1788. Graceful bell towers flank the convex, three-part façade. Inside, powerful columns divide the three naves, and the high altar of marble and alabaster is one of many priceless works of art.

West of Puerto

After you've seen the botanical garden of Puerto de la Cruz you may think it's odd to travel more than 20 km (12 miles) westward just to look at a single tree. But few are disappointed, and just beyond this stop are some poignant volcanic souvenirs.

Icod de los Vinos

El Parque del Drago (dragon-tree park) is the name of the small, well-tended park surrounding the legendary tree of Icod, nearly 20 m (65 ft) tall. The ancient dragon tree (*Dracaena draco*) is so illustrious that it featured on Spanish banknotes of 1,000 pesetas. It may be hundreds of years old or, as is often claimed, 3,000 years old (though that is hardly likely). No matter, it was venerated by the Guanches long before the Spanish conquerors arrived.

Legend also surrounds a small statue occupying a place of honour in Icod's parish church of San Marcos Evangelista. It is supposed to have been discovered on the coast before the Conquest, making it Tenerife's oldest religious image. The church itself goes back to the late 15th century.

Garachico

Until 1706, Garachico was Tenerife's prime port. Then it was wiped from the map in a volcanic catastrophe that left scars still visible today. The good news is that the townsfolk, warned of the fiery river of lava descending on them, escaped with their lives; and the town they rebuilt on the small peninsula of cooled lava became a radiant example of urban planning.

Garachico peninsula was created by an 18th-century flood of molten lava.

In 1980 King Juan Carlos awarded Garachico the Gold Medal of Fine Arts for preserving the artistic and historic heritage from the days of post-eruption reconstruction.

Castillo de San Miguel

A rare survivor of the 1706 cataclysm, the Castle of St Michael was constructed in 1575. Nowadays it is used for art exhibitions. The flat roof is a good vantage point for taking in the full scope of the disaster. Below the castle, natural pools in the volcanic shore permit refreshing bathing, unless the tides are too fierce. Whether you look at the tidy white town from the highway on the hills above or up close in the cobbled streets lined with historic mansions, churches and official buildings, you'll be impressed by Garachico's resilience and good taste.

Buenavista

Tenerife's westernmost town, Buenavista, is surrounded by impressive mountain scenery. A slender belfry announces the church of Nuestra Señora de los Remedios, built in the 16th and 17th centuries. (The belfry is a 19th-century afterthought.) Apart from the paintings and sculptures on view in the church, there is a

23

museum of religious art in the sacristy.

The end of the line, where the road westward runs out, is Punta de Teno. Connoisseurs of lighthouses will be pleased to find an old and a new lighthouse side by side. The view out to sea, predictably, is stirring.

Teide

Spain's most popular national park—with more than 3 million visitors a year—surrounds the nation's highest peak, Mount Teide. Sulphurous fumes seep from the volcanic crater, but there seems to be little to worry about from that source: Teide hasn't blown its top since 1798. A greater cause for concern is what the tourists may have done to the volcano: the effect of all those feet trampling on the edge of the cone, and the loss of all the pebbles that were pocketed as souvenirs.

Reaching the Summit

A cable car (teleférico), inaugurated in 1971, goes almost to the top of Teide. It's still a hike from the cable car's upper terminus to the summit, so sturdy shoes are essential, but it's a far cry from real mountain-climbing. (Even so, visitors with cardiac, respiratory or mobility problems should not even think of attempting the ascent.)

Assuming the mountain is not covered with snow, you can enjoy the sight of the brave flowers and plants that grow wild from the grim volcanic terrain; many are found nowhere else. The longer view, if clouds permit, takes in the whole island of Tenerife, great sweeping seascapes, and all the other islands of the archipelago.

Visitor Centre

On the eastern edge of the park, which is officially called El Par-

---

STARING AT THE SUN

A startling sight jars the eastern approaches to the national park: the weird white towers belong to the Teide Observatory.

When the Canaries Astrophysical Institute began its studies in 1964, the altitude, clean air and comparative isolation seemed ideal for star-gazing. Since then, however, the lights of Santa Cruz and the resorts have interfered, so night skies are studied from La Palma. Here scientists from several countries work the day shift, analysing the sun and its atmosphere. Tours of the telescopes can be arranged, but long in advance.

24

que Nacional de Las Cañadas del Teide, a visitor centre operates at El Portillo. It offers exhibitions of geological samples, videos, maps, suggestions on guided and unguided walks, and advice in general—on the unique flora, birdwatching, geological studies, and how and where to watch the sunrise.

Another handy stop is the Parador Nacional, a government-run tourist hotel at an altitude of about 2,200 m (over 7,200 ft). The swimming pool is the highest in Spain. There are only 23 guest rooms, but transients can take advantage of the eating and drinking facilities.

Around the Coast

Detailed maps of Tenerife show dozens of *playas* (beaches) all around the coast, most with intriguing names. The truth, however, is that many of them are small, rocky coves, difficult to reach and rarely worth the trouble. The most appealing beaches—relatively spacious, swimmable beaches—are in the south.

On the way there from Santa Cruz, the motorway runs along-side a neat, whitewashed city, better known for its historic significance than its black volcanic beach. Candelaria is well worth a stop.

Candelaria

The enormous, unshaded open square facing Candelaria's modern cathedral is called Plaza Patrona de Canarias. The size of the plaza is exaggerated to allow space for pilgrims who come to honour the patron saint of the Canaries, the Virgin of Candelaria; the biggest concentration celebrates the feast of the Assumption in August.

Inside the church, the Virgin of legend, crowned and lavishly gowned and bejewelled, couldn't be presented in a more theatrical scene—in a gold-framed stage behind the altar. Surrounding this, a modern fresco full of adoring angels illustrates the story of Our

THE TWO BEST MUSEUMS There are more than a dozen museums around Tenerife, but the two most important are in Santa Cruz. The **Museo de la Naturaleza y el Hombre** studies Guanche civilization—from skulls to pottery. **The Museo de Bellas Artes** is a well-presented survey of Canaries artists and mainland Spanish masters.

As clouds embrace Mount Teide, lesser crags reveal the volcanic story.

Lady of Candelaria, proclaimed the archipelago's patron saint by Pope Clement VIII at the end of the 16th century.

Legend of Our Lady

At least a century before the Spanish conquerors arrived, the pagan Guanches came upon a Gothic statue of a mother and child that washed ashore here. With no hint of its Christian significance, the cavemen idolized the image, thus giving the first missionaries a headstart in converting the natives. The Spaniards built a small church to house the statue, but both were washed away in a 19th-century disaster.

The grand new basilica, in a sort of neo-colonial style, with a giant cupola crowned with a cross, is a mid-20th-century replacement, as is the present statue. The complexion of the Virgin, and the crowned baby she holds, is almost the same as the colour of the black volcanic beach just beyond.

Nine Statues

Between the plaza and Candelaria's black shingle beach stand nine startling statues, bigger than life-sized, promoting the "noble savage" image of the Guanches. They represent the nine *menceys* or tribal leaders who ruled Tenerife before the conquest. Dressed, some of them scantily, in animal skins, they carry spears, staves or primitive knives. Their faces (all sculpted from imagination) are hirsute and reasonably handsome by European standards, though one is bald. The beach, too, is idealized: it looks inviting but the tides can be dangerous.

Güimar Pyramids

Southwest of Candelaria, an ethnographical park has been designed around seven enigmatic stepped pyramids, built in a style similar to the those of Mexico, Peru and ancient Mesopotamia. They are precisely aligned according to the sunset on the summer solstice, and a stairway on the west side of each pyramid leads to a platform on the top. First thought to be just agricultural stone terraces, the pyramids were taken more seriously when Thor Heyerdahl showed interest in their construction. A small on-site museum presents evidence and arguments on their possible origin.

El Médano

Queen Sofía herself dedicated the airport named after her, sometimes known as Tenerife South. Charter flights account for 80 per cent of the several million passengers arriving here each year.

Almost directly underneath the airport's flight path, the fishing village of El Médano has been transformed into a small resort. The secret of its appeal is the sea breeze. El Médano is said to be one of the best windsurfing beaches in the Canaries—a big claim by any standard. International windsurfing competitions are held here.

At the opposite end of the runway, the fishing port of Los Abrigos concedes to tourism with a lineup of restaurants overlooking the sea. Locally landed fish top the menu.

Costa del Silencio

Between Los Abrigos and the romantically named Costa del Silencio, two golf courses green the desert. The Costa itself is a far-flung, low-slung *urbanización* in search of a beach. No matter, something is always going on, on or near the rugged volcanic coast, be it scuba diving, windsurfing, fishing, fitness classes, tennis, shopping, dining or dancing. The nearby fishermen's village of Las Galletas is all but unspoiled in spite of the encroaching tourist developments.

Megatourism

The difference between Los Cristianos and Playa de las Américas, the shoulder-to-shoulder resorts on Tenerife's southwest coast, is that Los Cristianos was an actual fishing port long before the first tourist developer was inspired to exploit the beach. Fishing boats still bob in the bay at Los Cristianos, and the nautical life has taken on new intensity with the expansion of ferry and jet-foil service to the neighbouring island of La Gomera, in addition to a variety of excursions for fishing, whale-watching or fun.

Whereas Los Cristianos began as a real village, the *urbanización* of Las Américas was founded on nothing but dreams. For practical purposes, though, they are inseparable—a Tenerife version of Andalusia's Costa del Sol, but with guaranteed sunshine.

Los Cristianos

The name of the main street, Avenida de Suecia, salutes the strong contingent of Swedish tourists. From here down the hillside to the ocean a pedestrians-only area bustles with souvenir shops, restaurants, bars, a few hotels and many holiday flats. Some of the architecture still reminds the visitor of the village's origins. The beach, which starts almost alongside the fishing and ferry port, has been expanded and upgraded with imported sand, and swimming is safe for children. There's even a lifeguard station.

Playa de las Américas

North of Los Cristianos, a blinding white mirage spreads across the desert: the tourist metropolis of Playa de las Américas. The coastal strip of hotels was so successful that the bonanza has spread inexorably up into the barren hills—even to the edge of the motorway. Wherever the tourist alights, everything is close at hand, from supermarkets and discos to just-like-home "ethnic" restaurants (Swedish if you're Swedish, German for the Ger-

---

THE THREE BEST CHURCHES Almost every Tenerife church has architectural, artistic or historic merit, but here are three you shouldn't miss. By coincidence they are all called Iglesia de la Concepción. **Santa Cruz de Tenerife**: the capital's cathedral-like monument; **La Laguna**: a national treasure from 1497; **La Orotava**: a baroque masterpiece with lavish, elegant interior.

mans). The shoreline consists of a series of smallish beaches, protected by breakwaters, and a stylish marina called Puerto Colón in honour of Columbus.

Southern Diversions

Free enterprise has transformed some of the desert around the southern resorts into commercial recreation areas; you'll be deluged with brochures and face-to-face salesmanship.

Attractions include a comprehensive cactus garden, a banana plantation, a go-kart race track, and a waterpark with elaborate slides and pools. Among the infinite nightlife possibilities, Playa de las Américas has a fully-fledged casino.

Up the West Coast

From the southern resort complex a first-class two-lane highway, flanked by tomato and banana greenhouses, goes most of the way up the west coast. A few small resorts are signposted; some are destined for more intense development. The fishing village of Playa de San Juan has grown into a centre of holiday flats and villas. The same phenomenon is changing the pace in the seaside village of Alcalá. Award-winning Playa de la Arena has more beach front than most resorts along this coast, and it is framed by a dignified prom-

---

EYES ON THE AMERICAS

The name chosen for Playa de las Américas acknowledges the enduring links between the Canaries and Latin America. There has been so much interchange of people, commodities, language and ideas since the 16th century that a Tenerife newspaper (El Día) runs a daily page devoted to news from Venezuela, titled "The Eighth Island".

---

enade; the sand is unaffectedly black. Puerto de Santiago is a busy tourist spot just south of Los Gigantes. The big free bonus at the west coast resorts: sunsets.

Los Gigantes

Los Gigantes (the giants) is the name of a dramatic cliff side plunging about 450 m (nearly 1,500 ft) into the ocean. Los Gigantes is also the name of a small, fashionable resort snuggling up to the cliffs; the view is powerful, perhaps intimidating. For even greater impact you can take a boat trip into the shadow of the precipice and study the strata in the great wall.

Water sports like swimming, yachting, fishing and scuba-diving occupy the visitors when they are not shopping, drinking, eating or gazing at the cliffs. 29

LA GOMERA
San Sebastián, Villages and Landscapes

After a few hectic nights sampling the fleshpots of Playa de las Américas, the exhausted celebrant or repentant sinner may be ready to trade the desert sunshine of southern Tenerife for a visit to the cool, misty forests on the almost beachless neighbouring island of La Gomera. From Los Cristianos it's scarcely half an hour by hydrofoil, or 90 minutes by car ferry. Until a commercial airport becomes operational on Gomera—construction is under way—sea transport is the only means of getting there. Many island-lovers consider this a blessing: the only Canary without an airline connection is all but unspoiled. Although tourism is a minor factor in the Gomera economy, it has had a reverse effect: many islanders have moved over to Tenerife to work in the tourist industry there, keeping alive a long history of emigration.

Small and Round
Like Gran Canaria, La Gomera is almost circular in shape. It lacks the volcanic cones and badlands familiar elsewhere in the archipelago; Gomera's eruptions were finished a couple of million years ago. The island's area is nearly 370 sq km (143 sq miles). On the ground, it seems much bigger than the statistics indicate, for Gomera is so hilly and the roads so serpentine that it takes twice as long as you expect to reach any destination. Not that you'll be in a hurry—unless you have to catch the last boat to Tenerife.

Before the Spaniards
The aboriginal inhabitants of La Gomera, called Gomeros, lived a caveman existence similar to that on the other Canaries. Some particularities: they believed in one god (and one devil), they didn't go in for mummies, and they knew how to swim. Gomera was divided into four regions, each ruled by a prince. Native disunity eased the task of the Spanish conquerors, although the final subjugation of the Gomeros wasn't achieved until late in the 15th century, and at considerable cost to the underdog islanders.

Uneasy Colonization
The natives were still surly in 1492 when Christopher Columbus, bidding farewell to the known world, stopped at Gomera on the way to what turned out to

White houses and green banana plants clothe a fertile hillside in Gomera's valley of Hermigua.

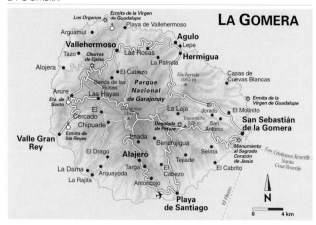

be America. For years the island's problem had been Fernán Peraza, the despotic Count of Gomera, an overlord who held himself remote from almost all of his subjects. A solution to the problem finally presented itself to the Gomeros shortly before the Columbus visit. The Count is remembered today in the evocative name of a mountain pass: La Degollada de Peraza (The Beheading of Peraza).

Columbus Days

The haughty Peraza was enjoying his *droit du seigneur* with a native princess. One night, as he left a tryst with her in a Gomera cave, he was murdered by out-
raged members of her family.

The Count was survived by a beautiful widow, Beatriz de Bobadilla, who disappeared from public view in the stark Torre del Conde (Count's Tower) in the port of San Sebastián de la Gomera. Gossip says that Columbus could have helped assuage the widow's grief. We may never find out how well they knew each other, but perhaps it was no coincidence that the Great Navigator kept coming back to Gomera—in 1492, '93 and '98.

Restoring Order

After the Count's assassination, Spanish troops were despatched from Gran Canaria to restore order and punish the guilty Gomeros. The occupation army

32

hanged many suspects and enslaved others in a reign of terror so cruel, even by the standards of the time, that the local bishop appealed to Ferdinand and Isabella to call it off. After a royally sponsored enquiry was convened, many of the deported Gomeros were returned to their island. At the end of the 15th century Gomera and the other islands came under the direct control of the Spanish crown.

San Sebastián

Your first port of call will be San Sebastián de la Gomera, the island's capital, where Columbus left his mark. The connection is a source of civic pride, which is just as well, for there's not much else of interest here. La Gomera's real charms are beyond this dreary town, amid the green tranquillity of the interior.

Iglesia de la Asunción

The Church of the Assumption was still unfinished in 1492 when, according to local historians, Columbus went to mass here before undertaking his voyage of discovery. A plaque commemorates his visit. In the 16th century, the church was in the news again when pirates attacked it. Famous freebooters John Hawkins and Francis Drake tried, but they were repulsed; the islanders gave thanks by building the chapel of the Pillar. Construction of the essentially Gothic church went on in fits and starts, and two more naves were added to the original one. The project was completed in the 18th century with the now-sagging doors. Some worthy sculptures add distinction to the dimly lit interior.

Main Street

La Calle del Medio (centre street) is San Sebastián's main thoroughfare, and the site of most of its historic monuments. La Casa de la Aguada contains a well from which Columbus's crewmen stocked up with water for the trip; this, it is inscribed, is the

---

ABORIGINAL ECHOES

The topography of La Gomera, with the steepest valleys, has always been a handicap. But the aboriginal Gomeros solved the communications problem. They whistled, meaningfully, from crag to crag. A whistling language, *el silbo*, evolved, and it is still "spoken" by a small minority of islanders today. Is it an actual language, or does the whistling merely encode Spanish sounds? Whatever the niceties, a long-distance demonstration of *el silbo* is an eye-and-ear-opening introduction to the mysteries of La Gomera.

water that baptised America. Casa de Colón is supposed to be where the navigator slept when he wasn't aboard his ship, but in fact, it did not exist at the time. The building is used for exhibitions. Beyond the post office, the Ermita de San Sebastián is a 15th-century institution honouring the town's patron saint.

Torre del Conde

The Count's Tower, dating from the middle of the 15th century, is one of the oldest Spanish monuments in the archipelago. It was built by the father-in-law of Beatriz de Bobadilla, the desirable widow who took refuge in the tower after her husband's assassination. According to the rumour mill, Columbus used to have assignations with the countess behind these thick, silent walls. Later, the gold of the Indies was stored in the fortress in transit to Seville. The tower is protected as a national monument.

Clifftops

Overlooking the port, the Parador Conde de Gomera is a modern reproduction of traditional Canaries architecture. Because the hotel is so small (58 rooms) and

Far from the beachy image of the Canaries, fishermen exploit a rocky Gomera cove.

so desirable, accommodation is usually booked long in advance, but the parador is a good place for lunch or a drink or just a look.

Farther north, with its own perch above the ocean, the 16th-century Ermita de Nuestra Señora de Guadalupe is the headquarters of the island's patron saint. The image of the Virgin of Guadalupe is honoured in Gomera's main festival.

Villages and Landscapes

The main road northwestward from San Sebastián rises steeply in zigs and zags, but a tunnel cuts through some of the worst of it. The views are striking as the scene changes from the sunny southeast coast to the misty uplands punctuated by precipitous valleys.

Hermigua

The white houses of the agricultural town of Hermigua dominate a fertile valley that's the island's centre of banana production. In the 16th century the crop here was sugar cane, but slave labour in the West Indies undercut Gomera's production costs. Hermigua's parish Church of the Incarnation was built in the mid-17th century. At Los Telares craft centre you can watch the local women weaving rugs and blankets. The traditional pottery is also highly regarded.

35

Agulo

Overlooking the sea, and with an unimpeded view of Tenerife's Mount Teide, this village is another agricultural centre. In this dizzying setting, the crops growing in terraces vary with the altitude, from bananas and grapes to potatoes. In the heart of the village stands the Iglesia de San Marcos (St Mark's Church), overshadowed by a giant laurel tree. The big-domed church served as a mosque during a spell of occupation by invaders from North Africa in the 17th century.

Parque de Garajonay

UNESCO, a connoisseur of such things, has proclaimed Garajonay National Park a World Heritage site. What makes these 4,000 ha (nearly 10,000 acres) so precious is the unspoiled forest of mighty laurel and cedar trees, rising into the haze. The humidity carried by the trade winds condenses among the treetops, promoting vigorous growth. But in mid-summer be alert to a risk of forest fires. A visitors' centre dispenses information on the trees and advice on walks.

Vallehermoso

This is one of those administrative centres, small in population but overseeing a big slice of countryside. Vallehermoso, meaning beautiful valley, runs all the way from the north to the south coast. In its jurisdiction is Gomera's most dramatic coastline, the cliffs called Los Organos. Boat trips can be arranged to admire these immense basalt columns, shaped like the pipes of a surreal organ, rising some 80 m (260 ft) from the ocean. Vallehermoso also nurtures palm trees producing excellent dates as well as *miel de palma,* "palm honey".

Valle Gran Rey

The beautiful banana lands of Valle Gran Rey, leading to the small beaches of the west coast, have attracted foreign interest. Former hippies and other escapists from Europe, mostly Germans, gather here to treasure the green tranquillity—and to support the boutiques and exotic bars and restaurants.

Playa de Santiago

Conventional international tourism, at four-star prices, has come to La Gomera at Playa de Santiago, a sunny south coast resort with a pleasant beach alongside a traditional fishing port. The island's biggest hotel, with 434 rooms, follows Canaries architectural traditions and offers everything the holidaymakers on the bigger islands expect, from swimming pools to multiple-choice restaurants, bars and a disco.

LA PALMA

Juan Adalid
Don Pedro
Tablado
Garafía
San Antonio del Monte
Gallegos
Barlovento
Cueva de Aqua
Llano Negro
La Mata
Franceses
Las Cabezadas
Los Sauces
Buracas
Hoya Grande
Fuente de la Zarza
Laguna de Barlovento
San Andrés
Las Tricias
Casa Roque Faro
Las Lomadas
Puntagorda
Pico de la Cruz 2351 m
Ermita San Mauro
Roque de los Muchachos 2426 m
830
La Galga
El Granel
Tinizara
Caldera de Taburiente
Pico de la Cruz 2351 m
Puntallana
832
Los Brecitos 1190 m
Parque Nacional
▲ *Pico de la Nieve 2239 m*
Tijarafe
Cueva Bonita
Pico Bejenado 1854 m
Las Nieves
Tenerifa
Gran Canaria
Arecida
▲ *Tamarahoya*
Ermita Virgen del Pino 900 m
Cumbre Nueva
Santa Cruz de la Palma
Los Llanos de Aridane
Breña Alta
El Hierro
Puerto de Tazacorte
La Fajana
El Paso
832
San Isidro
San José de Breña Baja
Tazacorte
San Isidro
Todoque
Volcán de San Juan
Mazo
Cueva de Belmaco
Lavastrom des San Juan
▲ *Pico Birigoyo 1774 m*
San Nicolás
Cráter de Hoyo Negro 1871 m
La Sabina
Puerto Naos
832
Deseada II 1875 m
Malpaises
El Remo
Santa Cecilia
Tiguerote
Cumbre Vieja
Tigalate
Monte de Luna
Las Indias
Las Caletas
Fuencaliente
Roque Tenequia
Volcán de San Antonio 857 m
Volcán de Tenequia 439 m
Faro de Fuencaliente

N

0   8 km

LA PALMA

Santa Cruz de La Palma, National Park,
Around the Island

The semi-official slogan of La Palma is *"la isla bonita"*—the pretty island. What an understatement! La Palma is not merely pretty, it's simply gorgeous, as beautiful as any paradise isle in the world.

Everything you could want is here, except golden beaches, a deficiency that discourages mass tourist development. Instead of burning your skin in the sun, you can admire grandiose forests, verdant valleys, elegant architecture from Spain's Golden Age, and the most striking vestiges of a violent volcanic past. There's nothing to worry about—La Palma hasn't seen an eruption since 1971.

Into the Clouds
The profile is extraordinary. With an area of 728 sq km (280 sq miles), it's only half the size of Rhodes or the Shetlands. But La Palma rises abruptly from the sea and attains the height of 2,423 m (7,950 ft), making it one of the steepest islands anywhere.

There are two visible benefits. The high-altitude posture attracts the moisture in the trade winds, assuring La Palma a plentiful supply of water: it's the only island of the archipelago with rivers and streams that flow year-round. The other advantage is that most nights the rain-rich clouds convene below the summit. This allows maximum visibility for the international array of telescopes on top—they comprise one of the world's leading facilities for studying the universe.

Conquest by Deceit
The troops of Alonso Fernández de Lugo invaded La Palma in September 1492. The story of the Spanish conquest here is rather less glorious than usual. It took more than seven months for European technology, tactics and, finally, treachery to overcome the aboriginal defenders of the island. The natives, called Auaritas, retreated to their redoubt in the Caldera de Taburiente, a huge volcanic crater. The invaders failed to dislodge them. Finally, they lured out the last resisting aboriginal king, Tanausú, by offering—word of honour—negotiations for peace. When Tanausú emerged he was ambushed and imprisoned; one version says he was shipped off to Spain, went on hunger strike, and died on the way. Thus ended the struggle for La Palma.

The Colonists

Sixteenth-century Europeans soon came to appreciate the possibilities of the northwesternmost Canary isle. Colonists arrived from Castille, Catalonia, Majorca, Portugal, Italy and the Low Countries. The few surviving Auaritas were integrated into the society. Agriculture thrived, with sugar the prime crop and wine a welcome addition. The forests provided timber for shipbuilding, and the port of Santa Cruz became an important stop on the new transatlantic trade routes. The heart-shaped island soon caught the eye of pirates. In 1553 the French freebooter known as Jambe de Bois (Pegleg) invaded and sacked Santa Cruz. The island's capital was rebuilt in a dignified, coherent style, creating a monumental ensemble admired to this day.

Agriculture Evolves

Sugar turned bitter when the West Indies took over the European market. Thanks to international feuding and changing tastes, the wine trade declined. For about half of the 19th century the big crop was cochineal, a dye derived from insects feeding on cactus. When that, too, proved a bust (with the invention of chemical dyes) the monoculture of La Palma switched to bananas. They are still most highly regarded, but the farmers hedge their bets with crops like avocados, potatoes, flowers and tobacco. Tourism is only a junior partner in the island's economy.

Santa Cruz de La Palma

The prettiest island has the prettiest capital. In Santa Cruz de La Palma (population 18,000) the traditional and the modern coexist, and everything is bright and cheerful. Whether you walk up from the port or take a bus or taxi from the airport, you'll be immersed in the mood within minutes.

Turn Right at the Fountain

Starting at the huge, modern, illuminated fountain in Plaza de la Constitución, Calle O'Daly, a pedestrian street, runs parallel to the seafront. O'Daly, of Irish origin, was a leading figure in the Canaries banana trade. On this street the most successful merchants of the prosperous 17th and 18th centuries built their mansions. One of the outstanding buildings is the palace of the Counts Salazar, a 17th-century refinement.

Plaza de España

The finest collection of religious and civic buildings from the 16th century surrounds Plaza de España, a triangular plaza of exceptional harmony.

The Church of the Saviour (Iglesia de El Salvador) was built in 1503, but only the Renaissance façade survived the raid by the pirate called Pegleg. The restored interior is notable for the wood ceiling, a Mudejar (Moorish-style) intricacy of geometric designs.

The plaza's hypotenuse is occupied by the Renaissance-style town hall with four arches, above which a bust of King Philip II recalls the building's dedication in the mid-16th century. A ceremonial staircase ennobles the interior. Neighbouring buildings are historic mansions.

A Ship Ashore

Along Avenida Marítima, traditional balconied houses overlook the seafront. These are the most typical of Canaries buildings, their weathered wooden balconies, painted green, sagging with age but rich in charm. A startling addition, beyond, is a full-sized, 20th-century replica of Columbus's *Santa Maria,* otherwise known as the Barco de la Virgen. Within, a naval museum is stocked with ship models, maps and memorabilia. Columbus's connection to La Palma is vague at best: as far as we know he never set foot on the island. But he docked elsewhere in the Canaries and, even at a distance, remains a local hero.

MAPMAKER'S HEADACHE

Do the Canaries confuse you? Feel no shame if you mix up La Palma with Las Palmas, the capital city of Gran Canaria. The capital of La Palma is Santa Cruz; the capital of Tenerife is also called Santa Cruz. One last complication: the very formal name for La Palma is San Miguel de la Palma. The aborigines called their island Benahoare.

Las Nieves

"The Snows" is a strange name for a village just uphill from the port of Santa Cruz, but it refers to the island's patron saint, Nuestra Señora de las Nieves—the Virgin of the Snows. The snows in question are supposed to have fallen in Rome one August day in the 4th century, accompanied by an apparition of the Virgin Mary.

The 17th-century church, with a Canaries-style balcony on its façade, is the home of a small terracotta sculpture of the Virgin of the Snows. Every year, in August, the lavishly robed and jewelled image is taken out for a procession that attracts big crowds. Every five years (2000, 2005, etc.), in an outpouring of devotion, the statue is carried down to Santa Cruz—the supreme festival of La Palma.

41

National Park

Beauty, tranquillity and mystery—and invigorating pine-scented air—pervade the Parque Nacional de la Caldera de Taburiente. The national park covers 4,690 ha (nearly 11,600 acres) of the centre of La Palma, offering spectacular mountain views, waterfalls, and impressive evidence of the savage force within a volcano. "Caldera" is the Spanish word for cauldron; its universal geological meaning— a very large crater, the remains of a collapsed volcanic cone— can be traced to the Canary Islands.

Into the Crater

From lookout points on the rim of the crater you can gauge the immensity of the geological event that took place hundreds of thousands of years ago: the caldera is 9 km (nearly 6 miles) across, and up to 700 m (2,300 ft) deep. At the bottom of the crater, a monolith called la Roque de Idafe was worshipped by the abo-rigines, and this is where their king, Tanausú, was besieged. Being here is a stimulating experience for ethnologists, botanists, vulcanologists and mountaineers, as well as ordinary tourists. You can enter the crater by car or by foot. The state of the roads may be a cause for concern but not the volcano; it has been extinct for a long time.

Hello, Universe!

The topmost point of La Palma bears the curious name of El Roque de los Muchachos (The Boys' Rock). Above the clouds, remote from the distractions of city life—air pollution, electronic interference and car headlights— astronomers and other scientists from all over Europe gather at giant telescopes to study outer space.

The experts consider this the clearest piece of sky on earth. They are not only seeing stars and sunspots but going after cosmic rays, quasars, black holes and all the other aspects of the universe.

4

THE FOUR BEST VOLCANOES La Palma's **Caldera de Taburiente** is as impressive as any volcanic relic anywhere. Of more recent vintage, **Teneguía** (1971) provides moving memories. Elsewhere, volcano fans won't want to miss Tenerife's **Las Cañadas del Teide** and **El Golfo**, on El Hierro.

It's an odd place to stumble on the astrophysical summit of Europe, weird sky-watch structures and all. Outside their observatories, the astronomers have a grand view over La Palma and the Atlantic, as well.

Around the Island

On the opposite side of the island from Santa Cruz, the second biggest town is Los Llanos de Aridane. Surrounded by banana plantations in a peaceful valley, the whitewashed city spreads from Plaza de España, a restful meeting place beneath the shade of the giant laurels.

To the southwest, the fishing port of Tazacorte came under the jurisdiction of Los Llanos until a royal decree of 1925. Tazacorte's black sand beach is where the Spanish conquerors came ashore in 1492.

Puerto Naos

Farther south, Puerto Naos has the only beach in La Palma big enough to support serious tourist development—albeit a very modest answer to Tenerife's mega resorts. Fringed by young palm trees, the fine black sand beach dips very gradually into the Atlantic, and the seas are usually calm. Inevitably, tourist development is expanding though it is still insignificant by Tenerife standards.

Fuencaliente

Near the southern tip of the island, the small town of Fuencaliente (meaning hot springs) is a brave survivor of La Palma's last volcanic eruption, dated 1971. Because there was advance warning that Teneguía was going to erupt, the townsfolk were able to escape with their lives. The lava reached as far as the coastline, but once it had cooled down, the "Fuencalenteros" turned the disaster into success, planting vines that now produce some of the best wines in the Canaries. Fuencaliente has a wine harvest festival in August. Nearby, the San Antonio volcano blew its top in 1677.

Cueva de Belmaco

Just south of the airport, the Belmaco Cave has intrigued generations of archaeologists and other investigators. The cave seems to have been a meeting-place, rich in religious and political significance, for the prehistoric Auaritas. The meaning of the cave inscriptions, in peculiar whirling designs, continues to resist all efforts at decoding. Much of the evidence was stolen or destroyed before the value of the inscriptions became evident.

Other locations of rock carvings are the grotto of La Zarza and the Roque de Teneguía, at Fuencaliente.

EL HIERRO
Valverde, East Coast, North Coast

As Columbus and his crew watched El Hierro fade into the horizon, they knew this was the real beginning of their adventure. All the experts agreed: anyone sailing beyond El Hierro would fall off the map into the unknown, the domain of demons, storms and unimaginable dangers. El Hierro, the westernmost Canary, had always been regarded as the last stop, the end of the world. Ptolemy said so in the 2nd century AD and nobody had contradicted his erudite ruling.

As you approach El Hierro, by sea or air, the end-of-the-world feeling might overtake you. Windswept and guarded by steep cliffs, it looks unapproachable, perhaps unliveable. Persevere and you may find it a perfect little getaway isle.

Meridian Zero

"Longitude zero" slices through the observatory at Greenwich, England. You can't tell the time without it. Greenwich Mean Time (GMT) is based on the sun's position over Greenwich. It wasn't always thus. In 1634, the world's geographers and astronomers proclaimed the precise location of Meridian Zero to be Punta Orchilla, the westernmost extremity of the Canaries.

Today a 20th-century lighthouse at Punta Orchilla flashes reassurance far into the Atlantic. But the world no longer ends, or starts, at El Hierro.

The Bimbaches

The aboriginal people of El Hierro, called Bimbaches, were peaceful cavemen ruled by a single king. Early in the 15th century, the Norman Conqueror, Jean de Béthencourt, convinced the king of the Bimbaches, Armiche, to submit to European rule. The takeover was nonviolent. Beyond its strategic location, the island was no huge prize for the conquerors. Slave labour was unenthusiastic, and there was never a dependable water supply. Nobody would predict a brilliant future for the smallest, least populous Canary, not even today.

Valverde

The capitals of all the other Canary Islands are established at sea level, where commerce and politics meet in a port city. El Hierro, remembering pirate attacks, keeps its capital on a mountainside. It's just as well, for the island has no port city worthy of the role. High above the Atlantic, Santa María de Valverde, to use the town's full name,

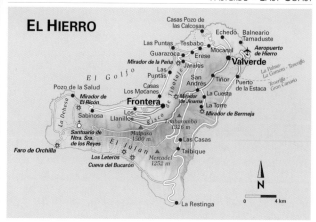

EL HIERRO

Casas Pozo de
las Calcosas
Echedó   Balneario
Tamaduste
Las Puntas   Tesbabo
Mocanal   Aeropuerto
Guarazoca   Erese   de Hierro
Mirador de la Peña   Jarales   Valverde
Las
El Golfo   Puntas   San   Tiñor   La Palma - Tenerife
Pozo de la Salud   Casas   Andrés   La Cuesta   Puerto   Tenerife
Mirador de   Los Mocanes   Frontera   Mirador   de la Estaca   Gran Canaria
El Ricón   de Jinama   La Torre
Sabinosa   Los   Mirador de Bermeja
Llanillos   Tibataje
Santuario de   Malpaso   Timbarombo
Ntra. Sra.   1500 m   1326 m
de los Reyes   El Julan   Las Casas
Faro de Orchilla   Taibique
Los Leteros   Mercadel
Cueva del Bucarón   1252 m

N
0   4 km

La Restinga

is as modest as its population—
fewer than 4,000 inhabitants.

Iglesia de la Concepción

While the pirate threat lasted,
the belfry of the Church of the
Immaculate Conception doubled
as a watchtower. A narrow balcony, suitable for a sentry's vigil,
surrounds the bell level of the
whitewashed tower. The clock is
a later addition, imported from
France in 1876. The church has
three naves and a baroque altar-
piece and other statues and treasures from the 18th century. From
the multilevel plaza descending
to the church there's a fine view
of its setting and the sea and, on a
clear day, Gomera and Tenerife's Mount Teide.

Two Museums

The island museum, next to the
tourist office, has exhibits on El
Hierro's archaeological discov-
eries and the culture of the aboriginal Bimbaches. On the way
out of town the Museo Juan
Padron, a private museum, houses
an eclectic collection of Canaries
antiques.

East Coast

Beaches are meagre in El Hierro,
but some protected coves provide
a welcome diversion on a warm
day. Northeast of Valverde, the
fishing village of Tamaduste has
the air of a seaside resort and
some facilities, even though the
actual stony beach is small. The
terrain is strictly volcanic bad- 45

Belfry looks down at its church, and out to sea, at Frontera, El Hierro.

lands. Down the coast, beyond the airport, La Caleta is another lava-created swimming zone, popular with the islanders. Not your obvious choice for a dip, Puerto de la Estaca is El Hierro's commercial port, a rather gloomy introduction to the island for ferry passengers and the crews of inter-island freighters.

Parador Nacional

The island capital is on a mountainside, but the Parador Nacional de Turismo is down by the sea on a black sand beach. The lonely location, called Las Playas (the beaches), is at the edge of a volcanic crater that has dropped into the ocean; the cliff side behind it was part of the cone. It's a long way from any place, but quite self-sufficient with all comforts, especially tranquillity.

Pinelands

Splendid views of the parador's situation can be seen from the heights above, where there are two lookout points, the Mirador de Isora and the Mirador de las Playas. These are in pine country, a refreshing attraction of the east-coast uplands.

At 34 km (21 miles) from Valverde, La Restinga is the southernmost village of El Hierro, and a principal fishing port, enjoying a new vocation for tourism. Most of the holidaymakers here are Germans or Scandinavians or scuba divers.

North Coast

El Hierro is well supplied with lookout points for admiring the scenery. Best of all, a few miles west of Valverde, is the Mirador de la Peña, a cosy vantage point overlooking El Golfo, a stupendous volcanic phenomenon. The mirador, designed by César Manrique, includes a first-class restaurant. The view takes in the 14-km (9-mile) semi-circular sweep of El Golfo, the inside of a defunct volcanic crater; the other half has long since subsided into the ocean.

Los Roques de Salmor

Another sight to savour from the mirador: the Salmor Rocks, offshore isles that used to be the home of a species of giant lizard. The Bimbaches kept their distance but the conquering Spaniards hunted the lizards, seriously reducing their numbers. In modern times it was presumed that the last lizard had already been taken for a trophy. But it now appears the pessimism was exaggerated, for they've been sighted on the "mainland" of El Hierro—not as enormous as their prehistoric ancestors but still as big as young alligators.

HONOURING THE VIRGIN

Towards the western extremity of El Hierro, on a difficult road, a shining white hermitage is the headquarters of the island's patron saint, Nuestra Señora de los Reyes (the Virgin of the Kings). The venerated statue is said to have been given to the islanders by the crew of a ship becalmed just offshore in the 16th century. Every four years the image, on a mobile throne of silver, is carried all around the island in a fiesta that lasts a whole month. Make a date for June 2001.

Pozo de la Salud

They've been drinking the water from the Well of Health since at least the 17th century, but its powerful properties became known much later. The boom came in the late 19th century, long after spas became popular in Europe. Health faddists continue to swig the warm water, in great quantities, soak in it, and wait for relief.

By way of inspiration to the ailing, El Sabinar, to the west, is a forest of gnarled and stunted juniper trees. They got that way by resisting the wind in a permanent struggle for survival. It looks as if the brave trees are winning.

CULTURAL NOTES

Aborigines

Telde, Taganana, Tagaluche, Teguise, Tindaya, Taibique and Tahuya are typical Canarian place names, one from each island. They all start with "T", and they were named by the original Stone Age inhabitants of the archipelago. These enigmatic people, who were absorbed into the mainstream of the Canarian population after the arrival of the Spaniards, continue to fascinate all manner of scientists, such as archaeologists, anthropologists and ethnologists. A German anthropologist went so far as to analyse the blood type of ancient corpses, discovering that 90 per cent had type O blood—an astonishing percentage almost anywhere except among the Berbers of North Africa. Just one more clue as to the origin of the first Canarians.

Beetles

The ingredients list on the food or drink or cosmetic product you buy may speak of "natural (red) colouring" or it may be more specific: "Cochineal". A Canaries speciality, *cochineal* consists of the crushed bodies of insects that cling to cactus.

The islands experienced a cochineal boom in the 19th century, turning a pest into a blessing, but the bubble burst when chemical dyes were invented. Now that natural products are again in vogue, the ecologists are happy and the local bug industry is again looking strong. Have another Campari!

Clay

The aborigines produced some competent, graceful ceramic work. You can see the originals in museums, and copies in shops: figures of extremely fertile-looking idols, and utilitarian or decorative pots and jugs. Considering that they had no potters' wheels, the caveman ceramists did very well with their hands-on technique, which is perpetuated to this day in some Canaries workshops.

Fiestas

When you stumble on a village fiesta, the locals may be celebrating the harvest or a civic anniversary but it's more likely to honour a saint. Since many towns have two patron saints, male and female, commemorated on different dates, you have twice the chance of seeing the faith in action. (The religion of the islands, as of mainland Spain, is overwhelmingly Catholic.)

There may be barbecues, fireworks, sports events and dancing on the fringes, but the fervent religious devotion of the hardcore celebrants is touchingly clear to see.

Music

The folk music of the islands is light and cheerful, the songs simple, with lyrics about everyday life and love—even, perhaps, something ironic about the tourist invasion. Canaries voices are youthful, energetic and unsophisticated. In brightly coloured costumes, unique to each island, the dancers swirl through complicated rounds. The accompaniment is led by the *timple*, a five-stringed instrument similar to a ukulele, and guitars and mandolins of various sizes.

Noise

Like most Spaniards, the Canarians enjoy being surrounded by noise of all sorts, especially the sounds of their own voices shouting across a crowded room in competition with a raging television set and a pneumatic drill digging up the street outside the window. They're not arguing, just chatting.

Rivals

Gran Canaria and Tenerife are as jealous as beautiful sisters. Many natives of one island have never visited the other, although it's only a 15-minute flight. When the internationally renowned Tenerife football (soccer) club plays, press coverage in Gran Canaria is minimal and critical. In Las Palmas de Gran Canaria you will search in vain for a map of Tenerife, and vice versa.

San Borondón

The Canaries archipelago consists of seven main islands plus six minor isles. Seven plus six equals 13, an unlucky number in some cultures. Is that why the Canarians talk about San Borondón, the legendary 14th isle? It's named after St Brendan, a medieval Irish monk who went to sea on the back of a whale in search of paradise. The story goes that the whale took him to the 14th Canary isle—or perhaps the whale itself was transformed into an island. Over the centuries sailors have claimed to have seen Brendan's little heaven-in-the-Atlantic, but the phantom isle has never officially been pinned down. You, too, can look for it: happy hunting.

Wrestling

Canarians like to say there's nothing in the world like *lucha canaria* (Canaries wrestling), a chivalrous sport handed down by the aborigines. Oddly, something very much like it seems to have been popular in ancient Egypt, and Swiss folklore to this day goes through similar motions in a sport called *Hosenlupf*. The Canaries wrestlers, barefoot, in short trousers rolled up at the cuff, also emphasize fair play and ritual; the winners are honoured as local heroes. *La lucha* goes on at every festival and the season lasts year-round, so you'll probably have a chance to see it. 49

Shopping

By royal decree in 1852, when transatlantic steamers were beginning to elbow aside the clipper ships, the Canary Islands were designated a duty-free area. It was good for business. In modern times the duty-free label provided an added incentive for the development of tourism. With Spain's entry into the European Union, however, the status had to be modified, and now the Canaries constitute a free-trade zone benefiting from a lower luxury tax than most places. Some real bargains are possible among certain ranges of products. You'll get the picture in the frenzy of any Tenerife shopping centre.

Imports

Audio and video equipment, calculators, cameras, watches and other imports can be attractive bargains in the Canaries. They can also, lamentably, be counterfeits, so you must be sure to ask for documentation, especially the manufacturer's international guarantee that goes with the genuine article. Merchants, who often hail from India or Morocco, assert that prices of Japanese goods are nearly as low as in Hong Kong, the distance making the difference. But haggling over the prices is part of the deal in these bazaars, and anywhere else that prices are not marked. During the bargaining process a 30 per cent reduction in the asked price can develop. Keep in mind that the merchants really expect you to negotiate.

Imported spirits and tobacco products, sold in supermarkets as well as the bazaars, are cheap by European standards; many of the best-selling international brands are involved.

Precious stones, uncut or in jewellery, are on sale; knowledgeable buyers can decide whether these are real bargains.

Island Products

Canaries artisans produce some desirable souvenirs, as serious as impeccably embroidered bedspreads or as simple as hand-carved toys.

Embroidered tablecloths, napkins, towels, handkerchiefs and so forth are a speciality of the islands, and tourist excursions sometimes go to workshops to see local women at their needlework. But beware of street mer-

After hearing the folk music, you might want to buy a Canaries guitar.

chants who may offer you cheap oriental substitutes under false pretences.

Island wines, the products of volcanic soil, are of high quality. They enjoy a certain snobbish appeal, but tend to cost more than imported vintages. Typical alcoholic souvenirs are banana liqueur, Canaries rum, and honey rum.

A souvenir of the taste of the Canaries is *gofio,* the islands' staff of life, for sale in small gift-sized sacks. They also bottle *mojos,* sauces more or less piquant, and the popular creamy dessert of eggs, almonds and honey called *bienmesabe.*

Tobacco is a standard crop, and hand-rolled cigars from La Palma are highly regarded. Tourist shops sell giant cigars, as well, for jokey gifts.

Hand-made pottery comes in original modern designs or reproductions of aboriginal treasures.

Wickerwork in many forms, from sombreros to serving trays, occupies the artisans in remote areas.

They also sell seeds, so you can try to grow your own strelitzia "bird of paradise" flowers or, for that matter, a dragon tree in your garden. You can also buy a fresh strelitzia at the last minute, specially packed for air travel.

Dining Out

From Argentine churrasco to Belgian waterzooi, the food in the major resorts is as cosmopolitan as the holidaymakers themselves. Eateries of German, Dutch, French, Hungarian, Scandinavian and Chinese persuasion allow the adventurous diner to explore the world in the microcosm of the Canary Islands. Hidden among the sophisticated international establishments are genuine Spanish restaurants, often run on regional lines by homesick Basques, Galicians and Madrileños. Some fine gastronomic experiences await. Even less obvious are the typical Canarian restaurants. No visit to the islands would be fulfilling without a sampling of authentic local fare, fresh, wholesome and usually delicious.

Meal Times

Breakfast in some of the tourist complexes is a big production—enormous buffets to suit the tastes of guests of various nations, with juices, fresh fruit, cereals, pastries, cold meats, eggs, cheese, coffee and tea. It's copious enough to cover lunch as well. In the towns and commercial centres, specialist cafés also aim at foreign tastes, for instance eggs, bacon and toast in the English style. But at the typical local café, the notion of breakfast is more spartan—coffee and pastry or toast on the run.

A pleasant surprise: lunch and dinner start earlier than in mainland Spain. Lunch hour is around 1 p.m. and dinner is under way by 8 p.m.

Canaries Cuisine

The usual way to start lunch is with a *sopa de pescado* (fish soup) or the hearty *potaje canario*, so thick you might mistake it for a stew. The ingredients can include chickpeas or lentils, potatoes, carrots, cabbage, a chunk of meat, perhaps a thin slice of corn on the cob. In restaurants it is no longer thickened with *gofio,* the all-purpose toasted, milled grain —wholemeal or maizemeal— handed down from prehistoric times. But this ancient island recipe sometimes features as *gofio escaldado*: a thick soup with the consistency of porridge.

Puchero canario is a stew more or less in the Spanish tradition except that the emphasis is on the vegetables, such as potatoes, sweet potatoes, cabbage, pumpkin, carrots, peas, chick-peas, onions and tomatoes. Lesser roles are played by whatever meats happen to inspire the cook at the moment—chicken, beef, lamb, sausages or bacon. A similar concoction goes by the enchanting name of *ropa vieja* ("old clothes"), in other words, the art of using up leftovers.

Papas arrugadas ("wrinkled potatoes") are served with many dishes. These small, tasty tubers are boiled in heavily salted water and eaten jacket and all, with the addition of a *mojo* sauce. The red sauce—*mojo rojo* or *mojo picón*—is made from garlic, olive oil and vinegar spiced with turmeric and thyme and bristling with hot chilli peppers. The much milder green sauce, *mojo verde*, relies heavily on parsley for flavour and colour. These sauces are often presented on the table, suitable for enlivening fish and meat dishes and almost anything else; don't fail to try them, you'll never ask for ketchup again.

Fish and Seafood

Surrounded by seas rich in fish, the islanders have always consumed the harvest of the Atlantic. The aborigines, who didn't know much about boats, engaged in a bit of shore fishing but more commonly depended on a diet of shellfish, leaving small mountains of the shells for archaeologists to ponder. Nowadays the fishing boats return laden with trophies, from sardines to tuna. Curiously, dried and salted fish are also popular in Canaries recipes.

Sancocho uses salted sea-bass or cod as the basis of a rich winey stew containing onions, garlic, potatoes, sweet potatoes and other vegetables, and heavily influenced by *mojo verde*.

Turning to fresh fish which can be grilled or baked, look for Canaries specialities such as *vieja* (meaning old woman), actually a thoroughly delicious mid-Atlantic fish; *sama*, a big, tasty fish with flaky white meat; and *cherne*, a sort of grouper.

Seafood includes *mejillones* (mussels), *gambas* (shrimp), *calamares* (squid) and *langostinos* (king prawns), some local and others from faraway hunting grounds, depending on supply and demand.

Meaty Matters

You can find an Argentine steak or an American-style hamburger, but if you want to stick with Canary Islands cuisine look for *cordero* (lamb), *cabrito* (baby goat), *conejo* (rabbit) or *cochino* or *chicharrón* (pork). *Pollo* (chicken) is prepared in varied ways, such as *asado* (roasted) and *a la brasa* (grilled).

Desserts

Sweets are a local matter, varying from island to island and even within each island. Some are made only for special occasions, such as Carnival, Holy Week or village fiestas.

The most famous Canaries dessert has the bewitching name *bienmesabe*—meaning approximately "relish me" or "how tasty!" It's richer than you can imagine, composed of sugar, almonds, egg yolk, milk, lemon juice and cinnamon, with the possible addition of honey and a hint of wine or rum. If you like it, you can buy it by the jar to take home as a sweet souvenir. As everywhere in Spain, you'll be offered *flan*, egg custard with caramel sauce. Canarians also concoct a rice flan with honey (*flan de arroz con miel*), also in a mould.

El Hierro produces a mouthwatering mini-cheesecake called a *quesadilla*. La Palma's proudest desserts are little almond cakes, *almendrados*.

As a refreshing alternative to the creamy desserts, try fresh fruit: bananas, pineapples, mangos, papayas, figs—semi-tropical or not, whatever's in season.

Cheeses

Although cheese comes after desserts in our survey, the Canarians tend to eat theirs as a starter. Most of the Canaries cheeses are fresh and light, made of goat's milk or a combination of goat's and sheep's milk. Occasionally it is smoked or cured or flavoured with herbs. Canarians consume far more cheese per capita than Spaniards in general, and this in spite of the lack of a great variety from local producers. Hard cheeses from mainland Spain and other countries are also available.

Drinks

As they have been doing for centuries, all the Canary Islands produce wine, though you may have to hunt it down. Tenerife is the biggest winemaker, accounting for more than half the archipelago's total area of vineyards. The volcanic soil makes for some unique, earthy wines. Historically the sweet *malvasía* (malmsey) was identified with the Canaries, but modern producers have branched out into drier clarets, whites and rosés with lower alcohol content. In practice, most restaurants serve wine from mainland Spain, for it is cheaper and more abundantly available.

Canaries beers—*Tropical* and *Dorada*—are in the lager style and served ice cold. The familiar soft drinks are always available, or you can drink mineral water (*agua mineral*), fizzy or still (*con gas* or *sin gas*).Island distilleries produce rum, and fruit liqueurs based on bananas or honey.

Sports

From the traditional sailing and golf to contemporary sports like windsurfing, jet-skiing and hang-gliding, the Canaries keep sports-lovers busy and happy on land, on sea and in the air. The nice weather helps.

Water Sports

Every activity imaginable is available, starting with swimming. Tenerife's southern resorts are built around well-cared-for beaches where children can normally frolic in the ocean without any danger. But red flags mean the tides are unacceptable. Beyond the resorts, ask for local advice before plunging in. Where beaches are inadequate or unsafe, many resorts have improved their oceanside pools, refreshed with clean salt water at every high tide. The most elaborate man-made "costa" is at Puerto de la Cruz. On the islands west of Tenerife, swimming opportunities are limited.

Scuba diving

Tenerife's big resorts have diving schools and mount expeditions to interesting undersea areas.

Windsurfing

Beginners will find equipment, instruction and adequate breezes at the resorts. International competitions are held at windy El Médano, Tenerife. For old-fashioned surfing, Playa de Martiánez at Puerto de la Cruz, Tenerife, is a favourite hangout.

Sailing

Many transatlantic yachtsmen use Canaries ports for rest and recreation breaks between the Caribbean and the Mediterranean. Tenerife has a number of well-equipped marinas, from Santa Cruz to Los Cristianos and Playa de las Américas and around to Los Gigantes.

Deep sea fishing

Tuna, swordfish, shark, marlin and barracuda await the charter boats that depart from working ports and resort zones.

Land Sports

There's plenty to keep landlubbers happy, too.

Golf

A real fanatic could fly in to Tenerife, play golf to the point of exhaustion, and leave the island without ever doing anything else. The Tenerife Golf Club is conve-

At Playa de las Américas, the ocean beckons windsurfers and swimmers.

niently located near Los Rodeos airport. In southern Tenerife, the Amarillo Golf Club and Golf del Sur are both handily near the Aeropuerto Reina Sofía.

Tennis

All the big hotels and many of the apartment complexes have their own courts, many of which are lit for night play. Instruction is often available. Table tennis is also on the agenda.

Horse-riding

Stables near Santa Cruz, Puerto de la Cruz, and the Costa del Silencio offer instruction and excursions.

Hang-gliding

The foothills of Spain's highest mountain, Teide, are a memorable departure point for this uplifting sport. For details, check with a *club parapente*.

Spectator Sports

The complex, highly ritualized sport of Canaries wrestling, *lucha canaria*, an oasis of fair play in a ruthless world, is a popular attraction at every fiesta, all year round. Islanders also support more universal sports. Football (soccer) attracts big crowds, and increasingly the high-scoring spectacle of basketball has a lively following.

The Hard Facts

Airports
Millions of passengers smoothly transit the two main Canaries terminals, on Tenerife and Gran Canaria, which are spacious and efficient intercontinental airports. (Queen Sofía airport, sometimes called Tenerife South, is near the big resorts of Los Cristianos and Playa de las Américas. Tenerife's original airport at Los Rodeos, now called Tenerife North, is almost entirely dedicated to inter-island flights.)

The smaller islands have their own cosy airports, largely for inter-insular commuter flights and charters. The exception is Gomera, whose airport is not yet finished.

All the airports have the usual amenities—baggage trolleys, information desks, car hire counters, banks, post offices, bars and restaurants. Don't look for a duty-free shop; since prices on tobacco, alcohol and electronics are so low everywhere around the islands, it's wise to stock up before you reach the airport.

Climate
The famous "eternal springtime" is an over-simplification, but chances are good that the climate won't disappoint you. The ocean temperature, under the influence of the cool Canaries Current, is lower than you'd expect at this latitude; it contributes to the all-round mildness.

On the north coasts of all the islands the trade winds may bring showers or chilly "horizontal rain". The south coasts are warmer and sunnier. The archipelago's eastern islands may get uncomfortably hot on certain days of summer, when sun-baked, sandy air from the Sahara desert whooshes in. Generally speaking, it's warmer in Gran Canaria than in Tenerife and the western islands.

Some averages for Tenerife: 17°C (63°F) in January, 23°C (74°F) in July. Rainy days probable: seven in January, none in July.

Clothing
Casual dress is the norm, but you'll need modest clothes if you visit a historic church or a museum or official building. The nights can get chilly, so come prepared with a sweater, jacket or wrap. Sooner or later you may be grateful, too, to have brought along a raincoat. If you plan on 57

mountain climbing, stout boots and warm covering are essential.

Communications

The telephone service is good for local, inter-island and long-distance calls. You can dial an overseas number from any street-corner telephone, if you have enough coins or a phone card (*tarjeta telefónica*). Instructions are clearly indicated on the apparatus. For local numbers dial all nine figures.

If the prospect of running out of money or time—or the street noises—disturb you, go to one of the telephone centres operating in tourist areas. You dial your number yourself from a sound-proofed booth and pay the metered sum when you finish. Phoning from a hotel room can entail a surcharge, even if you dial it yourself.

Postal service. Every city and town has its post office, where you can buy stamps and post your letters and cards. Stamps are also sold at tobacconists and at many establishments that sell post cards. Spanish pillar boxes are yellow, and marked *Correos*. In big cities and resort centres there may be two slots—one marked *España* for domestic destinations, the other *Extranjero* (foreign).

Fax. Chances are your hotel has a fax on which you can send and receive written messages. Otherwise try the post office or one of the telephone centres.

Complaints

Hotels and restaurants everywhere in Spain have official complaint books. Just asking to fill out a complaint form will give you a certain influence on the management, which will probably prefer to solve the problem before anything drastic occurs.

If you think you've been overcharged or sold shoddy goods at a street market or one of the shops with negotiable prices, it may be too late to do anything about it. But if you feel strongly, take your complaint to the tourist office.

Crime

Burglaries have become commonplace in Canaries tourist centres, but the incidence of violent crime involving tourists remains reassuringly low. The tourism authorities urge visitors to keep all valuables in the hotel's safe. (If you're in a holiday flat be sure to lock doors and windows when you're out, and leave nothing valuable in view.) Mind your handbag and photographic equipment at the beach or in any crowded area; don't leave your wallet hidden under your towel when you go for a swim. Locking a car and leaving nothing useful in sight is another elementary precaution. On some islands stealing cars for joy-riding purposes is a popular pursuit of local youngsters.

A non-violent danger confronting many tourists is the old-fashioned swindle. Aggressive but personable salesmen for time-share properties accost visitors in their own language, promising the earth and inveigling them to sign contracts they may regret. Sign nothing until you've consulted your lawyer at home.

Currency

The Spanish *peseta* (abbreviated *pta.*) is the Canaries currency. There are coins from 1 to 500 pesetas and banknotes from 500 to 10,000 pesetas. Confusingly, a new generation of coins coexists with some old ones of different sizes and shapes. Well-known international credit cards are widely welcomed. Traveller's cheques and Eurocheques can be cashed at banks and exchange offices, and many banks have 24-hour automatic cash machines which dispense pesetas billed to your home bank or credit card. When you get home you may find that the service charge is significant.

Driving

Renting a car in the Canaries is straightforward and largely free of complications. Local compa-

nies compete with international firms at the airports and in towns and tourist centres.

The rules of the road follow European norms: drive on the right, overtake on the left. Maximum speed limit is 120 kph (74 mph) on the motorways, elsewhere 100 kph (62 mph) as marked. In built-up areas a limit of 60 or 40 kph (37 or 25 mph) is announced. All travel can be disrupted by construction work and repairs, and the impatient local drivers often take the law into their own hands. Other dangers: tourists pausing to read maps and road signs, and cyclists and joggers enjoying the great outdoors, even on motorways.

Petrol stations are well distributed. In city centres and beach-front areas many towns have installed parking ticket machines instead of meters. They are signposted by a symbol of a hand inserting a coin in a slot. The amount of time you buy varies, and there are many complexities in the rules, but all is explained on the machine. Display the ticket on your windscreen.

Emergencies

Throughout the Canaries the emergency number for municipal police is **091**. The Civil Guard answers when you dial **062**. But the best place to start is your hotel desk. In complex cases, consult 59 your consulate; they will be able to provide a temporary passport if yours is stolen, and can help you obtain money from home.

Essentials

Anything you forgot to pack can probably be bought on the spot; the shopping is quite civilized in the Canaries. But if you take prescription medicines, it's wise to pack all you need: it may not be easy to track down the Spanish equivalent in the correct dosage. And take along enough film for your camera. Restocking may be expensive on the spot. A wise precaution before leaving home is to make photocopies of your passport and plane tickets and keep them in a separate place.

Formalities

For most travellers, the only paperwork involved in going to Spain is the form for the immigration authorities which you fill out on the plane. Certain nationalities have their passports stamped on arrival and departure, but visas are not required for citizens of most of Europe, North or South America. At your hotel or holiday flat in the Canaries another form awaits; and the receptionist may hold on to your passport overnight, but it will be well looked after.

The airport customs officers normally wave everybody's baggage through without inspection. For practical purposes there are no restrictions on currency imports or exports, but if you plan to take in or out of the country more than a million pesetas or the equivalent in foreign money you're supposed to check in with the customs department.

Health

The salubrious climate and good standards of hygiene add up to a carefree outlook. When damage is done it's almost inevitably self-inflicted. To avoid sunburn, an uncomfortable and even dangerous fate, start the broiling slowly the first few days, avoid the hours when the sun is high in the sky, apply sunscreen, and wear a hat and a shirt. Another common problem is the standard hangover resulting from alcoholic excesses. The "duty-free" drinks are so cheap here that visitors from high-tax areas sometimes lose their heads. As for the water, it's drinkable, but many travellers are sensitive to changing bacteria and mineral counts, so bottled water is safer.

Residents of European Union countries are entitled to free medical treatment anywhere in Spain, including the Canaries, but you'll need an E111 form. For fewer bureaucratic complications, and to avoid hanging around over-stretched state-run hospitals, holiday health insurance is a prudent investment in private health care. It's even more so for residents of non-EU countries, who would be sent to private hospitals or doctors. The Spanish Red Cross runs a comprehensive ambulance service but there are private ambulances as well.

For minor health problems, any local chemist's shop will suggest a solution. Look for the green cross marking a *farmacia*. At least one chemist's in each city or major tourist centre stays open at night. The address is posted in the window of every other *farmacia,* or look in any local newspaper.

Holidays and Fiestas

Fixed public holidays are:

January 1	New Year
January 6	Epiphany
March 19	St Joseph's Day
May 1	Labour Day
July 25	St James's Day
August 15	Assumption
October 12	Columbus Day
November 1	All Saints' Day
December 6	Constitution Day
December 8	Immaculate Conception
December 25	Christmas

The movable feasts are Maundy Thursday, Good Friday and Corpus Christi.

In addition, every town has its own religious and civic fiestas scattered over the year.

Language

Except for slight differences of vocabulary, pronunciation and intonation, the language of the Canaries is the same as Castilian Spanish. Mainland Spaniards usually lisp when they pronounce the letters c and $z,$ but the Canarians, like Latin Americans, avoid this. In tourist areas, English and German are widely understood, with French a distant third. Signs and menus are written in many languages, including Swedish, Finnish and Dutch, and of course English and German.

Media

Leading European dailies and magazines are sold everywhere that tourists congregate, and in the languages of all significant groups of visitors. Most papers arrive at least a day late. Specialized local weekly newspapers and monthly magazines aimed at English and German tourists are published on several islands.

If your hotel room or holiday flat is equipped with a TV set you can pick up Spanish channels and, in some cases, satellite programmes in other languages, such as CNN and BBC Prime.

On radio, a short-wave transistor will pick up BBC, Voice of America and other international broadcasts. Some local radio stations have English and German programmes for tourists.

Opening Hours

Banks and post offices are usually open Monday to Friday from 8.30 or 9 a.m. to 2 p.m. and Saturdays until 1 p.m.

Shops generally observe the siesta, closing between 1 and 4 or 5 p.m., for a leisurely lunch and some relaxation, then reopening until 7 or 8 p.m. In the resorts some shops go nonstop from 9 a.m. to 9 p.m.

Photography

Taking pictures of military bases is forbidden. Some museums and churches ban photography. But along the road, a beauty spot or lookout point is usually indicated by a sign depicting an old-fashioned bellows camera.

If you want to take pictures of the local people it's polite to ask permission—if you can't handle the problem verbally, sign language will suffice.

Police

Each community has its local police force—normally in blue uniforms—to keep the traffic moving and maintain order. They may not speak your language but they are attuned to the problems of visitors and can be most helpful. The *Policía National* is a security and anti-crime force, and the *Guardia Civil* patrols the highways on powerful motorbikes.

Religion

Since 1482, when an aboriginal chieftain, Tenesor Semidán, asked for baptism before Ferdinand and Isabella, the Catholic Monarchs, the Canaries have had only one principal religion. Masses are said in churches all over the Canaries, many of them historical monuments.

There are Anglican churches in Santa Cruz de Tenerife and Puerto de la Cruz. In Tenerife's southern tourist zone, hotel bulletin boards announce local Protestant services.

Social graces

Don't try to revolutionize island life, with its unhurried pace. Things eventually get done, but not always on the first try. The more you fume at delays or apparent lack of interest, the worse the reaction will be from anyone living the *mañana* way. Relax, smile, and remember you're on holiday.

If you have children in tow, you'll find the islanders more than kind to them. Local toddlers are taken everywhere at all times of day and night, which might give your own brood some revolutionary ideas.

Time Difference

The Canaries are perpetually one hour behind mainland Spain and the rest of continental Europe, so it is always the same time as in Great Britain. The islands adhere to GMT in the winter, and advance clocks for daylight saving time in spring and summer. As in the rest of Spain, punctuality is not a pressing matter in the Canaries.

Tipping

Taxi drivers and hairdressers expect a tip of 10 per cent, waiters up to 10 per cent if you have been well served. When in doubt, do as you would at home. Don't forget some coins for hotel maids and porters.

Toilets

Public toilets are rare, so aim for the facilities in the nearest hotel lobby, restaurant or bar. The least you can do is order a coffee if you use a bar's toilets.

Transport

On the more developed islands the relatively cheap local and intercity bus service is a useful way to get around. All the bus lines on Tenerife are run by the TITSA organization. Trying to reach less obvious destinations takes some planning. The schedules and routes are on display at bus stops. You can buy your ticket from the driver.

Inter-island boats. Ferry-boats most days and jet foils several times daily link Tenerife and Gran Canaria. Several times a week there are sailings for La Palma. From Los Cristianos frequent daily ferries and hydrofoils go to Gomera, with ferries several times a week for El Hierro.

Inter-island flights. It's rarely more than a 20 to 30-minute flight between islands of the archipelago. There are a dozen or more daily flights from Tenerife to Gran Canaria. If you're skipping over an island or two, for instance, travelling between Tenerife and Lanzarote, the airline schedule is likely to be vastly more practical than any sea route.

Taxis. In cities and some tourist concentrations the taxis are metered. If not, the fare is regulated by a standard list of destinations (which are not subject to haggling). You can hail a taxi on the street—a green light or *libre* sign tells you it is free—or pick one up at one of the taxi ranks at hotels, bus stations or other crucial locations.

Voltage

With some 110-volt exceptions, the Canaries run on 220-volt 50-cycle AC voltage. When in doubt, ask at your hotel desk or holiday flat office before plugging anything in. Two-pin plugs are used, so you may need an adaptor if you have brought your hairdryer along.

INDEX

General editor: Barbara Ender-Jones
Photos: Bernard Joliat, Francis Brot, A.G.E. FotoStock, A. Taglicht
Maps: Elsner & Schichor; p.5 JPM Publications

Copyright © 1999, 1994 by JPM Publications SA
12 avenue William-Fraisse, 1006 Lausanne, Switzerland
E-mail: information@jpmguides.com
Web site: http://www.jpmguides.com/

Printed in Switzerland—Gessler/Sion (CTP)   Edition 1999–2000